I0560879

WORKBOOK

THE REBIRTH & REVIVAL OF A REBEL

A Practical Guide to Personal Restoration Based
On The Works Of Author & Pastor Jean Belizaire

Jean Belizaire

WORKBOOK

THE REBIRTH & REVIVAL OF A REBEL

A Practical Guide to Personal Restoration Based
On The Works Of Author & Pastor Jean Belizaire

Jean Belizaire

Books Academy LLC
112 SW H K Dodgen Loop
Temple, Texas 76504
Hotline: (254) 800-1189

Ordering Information:
Quantity sales. Special discounts are available on quantity purchases by corporations, associations, and others. For details, contact the publisher at the address above.

Printed in the United States of America.

ISBN-13:	Paperback	978-1-966567-36-3
	eBook	978-1-966567-37-0

Library of Congress Control Number:

Introduction

You are a vital part of what is called "The Critical Mass." This workbook is about intentionally using the critical mass to create miracles of self-restoration and positive impacts in your community.

The miracle of critical mass is the theory that supports the idea that subtle messages either consciously or subconsciously are passed down from one individual to another to create a belief-system that can either build a community or destroy the latter.

The thought of interest is that most people are not fully aware of the belief-systems that they have and the intricate role they play in one's thinking, communication, decision, and self-image.

This workbook is intentionally designed to both identify the systematic way of thinking one may have the liberate them using skillful and tried principles that will both deprogram and reprogram the human mind, creating what is termed as the miracle of the critical mass; because as one individual changes, he can change his community's mindset through inspired actions.

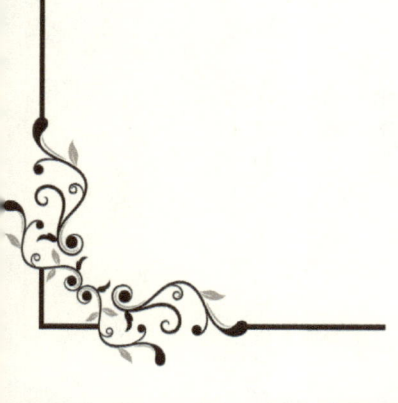

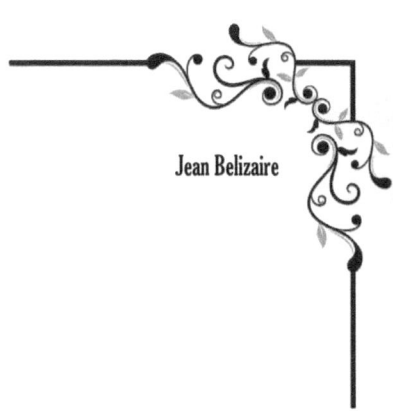

Jean Belizaire

SESSIONS 1

The influence of one's environment
on the human mind

MATTHEW 13: 3-8

ANALOGY:

- The individuals being the seeds
- The soil being various environments

STEP ONE: identification

- Identifying the root causes, and origins of systemic thinking and behaviors.

Facilitator: Jean Belizaire

Description:

The purpose of this session is to discover one's foundation of beliefs about oneself and others based on the type of parental experiences they've had, and the type of family upbringing that has set into a subconscious motion certain dynamic principles, values, and ideology that they have carried with them into their adulthood.

Workshop Setting:

Through a strategic art of group participation and storytelling, Pastor Jean Belizaire will be helping the audience or participant go through a dynamic mental detoxification from negative thoughts pattern.

Workshop Tools:

- Active Questioning
- Journaling
- Self-Awareness technique with eyes closed
- Excuse elimination
- Finding one's own internal power
- Letting go
- Changing perspective
- Story rewriting

ACTIVE QUESTIONING

What type of Father did you have?
-----Describe the good and the bad-----

How was your relationship with your father?
-----Describe the good and the bad-----

What are some of his traits you see in you?
-----Describe the good and the bad-----

What part of his life you wish you never have?
-----Describe the reason why-----

PS: If your father was absent you still must analyze impact of an *absent father* on your life; because that has contributed to shaping your self-image.

Journaling

- Write down 5 negative things that you believe your relationship with your father have caused in your mind

Workbook: The Rebirth and Revival of a Rebel

Jean Belizaire

STEP ONE: Reverse Psychology

- Reversing the subconscious desire to be a victim with no other alternatives.

Facilitator: Jean Belizaire

Description:

The purpose of this session is to reveal how humans can find comfort in victimization. When we accept our self-concept or self-image as a victim, we develop a subtle emotional comfort not to try to seek for alternatives to succeed and become better people. It's almost as if subconsciously we desire to fail so that we may have a reason to blame our misfortunes or the people who have wronged us. Reversing this subconscious self-programming is a powerful way to liberation.

Workshop Setting:

Through a strategic art of group participation and storytelling, Pastor Jean Beliizaire will be helping the audience or participants go through the power of reverse psychology that brings a mental liberation and an emotional freedom.

Workshop Tools:

- Active Reflection
- Acceptance of positivity
- Maximize positivity
- Creative writing
- Personal Vows

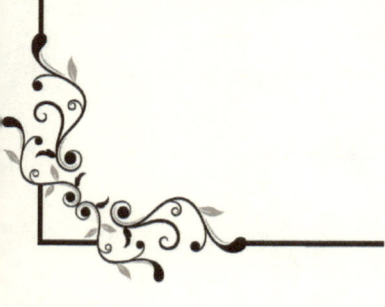

ACTIVE REFLECTION

Name 5 positive things that your relationship
with your father or your mother has caused
you to realize in your life:

*You will name one obvious thing, event, or fact.
Then you will name four non-obvious things,
events, or facts that came to you through self-
realization.*

How do you think your life will turn out to be if
those 5 positive ingredients were missing?

*You will now write a short to answer the
above question by associating facts to possible
outcomes based on assumptions.*

Create a short speech about any creative ways
you could use to enhance your awareness of
the above 5 positive ingredients of change.

PS: It is recommended to have the courage to
step out of your seat and stand in front of the
audience and share your writing or story.

Workbook: The Rebirth and Revival of a Rebel

_____

_____

_____

_____

_____

_____

_____

_____

_____

_____

_____

_____

_____

_____

_____

_____

_____

_____

_____

_____

_____

_____

_____

_____

_____

_____

_____

_____

_____

_____

_____

_____

_____

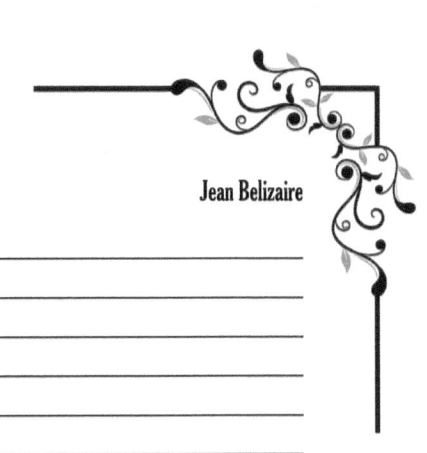

Jean Belizaire

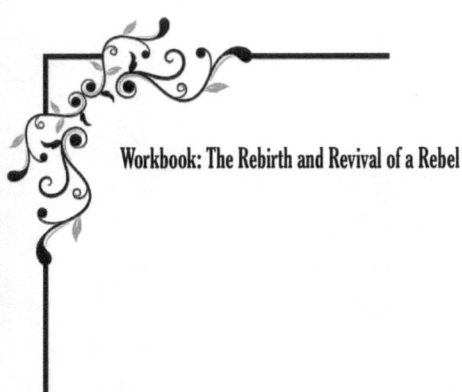

SESSIONS 2

The dominating power of the human
Mind over the environment

<u>MATTHEW 12:33</u>

ANALOGY:

- The individual is like a tree
- The individual can make himself good
  again and start producing good fruits

Jean Belizaire

STEP ONE: Reprogramming

- Using discoveries made in quantum physics and neuroplasticity to heal from past traumatic events.

Facilitator: Jean Belizaire

Description:

We often forget that the past is not in a time line but in the brain. Quantum physicists have proven time and time again that the brain does not know the difference between what you are imagining and what you are doing in real time. This explains the amazing truth found in neuroplasticity that we can change our brain. Using these two scientific discoveries, we can substitute the traumatic past with a better future by programming this future inside the brain.

Workshop Setting:

Through a strategic art of group participation and storytelling Pastor Jean Belizaire will be helping the audience or participant go through a dynamic mental detoxification from negative thoughts pattern.

Workshop Tools:

- Active Imagining
- Visualization
- Vision Board
- Goals Board
- Self-Talking using a mirror
- Daily commitment

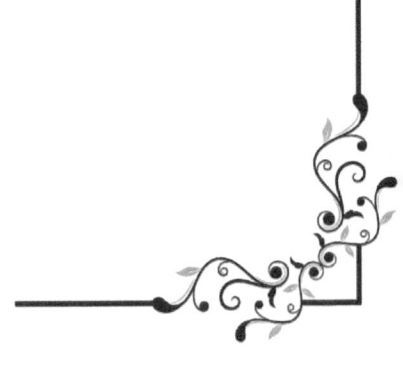

ACTIVE IMAGINING

Imagine your life without the traumatic past and describe the best version of a father and a mother you see in this imaginary life.

Write down the imaginary story

Come to the realization that your traumatic past is not real in this space time continuum. It is only in your imagination all these years. And you are the one giving it life by infusing it with feelings and emotions.

In this very second, is your father hurting you? No. In this very second, is your mother hurting you? In this very second is whatever negative event that happened to you happening now? No. So where is it? In your imagination. In the brain. Inside the mind.

You can decide to stop giving life to the painful past, right here and right now to free your brain? You can also decide to create in your imagination a better life until the brain fabricates the right chemicals that will become the supportive emotions to help you take the right actions to create it. Would you like to?

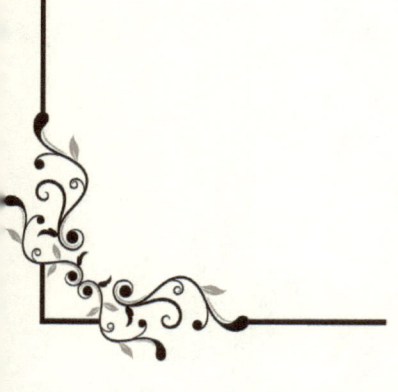

PS: Write the story of your best life you can imagine using your mind.

Journaling

- For the next 92 days you will rewrite the same story of your best life, keep editing it to make it better and read it to

Workbook: The Rebirth and Revival of a Rebel

Jean Belizaire

_____

_____

_____

_____

_____

_____

_____

_____

_____

_____

_____

_____

_____

_____

_____

_____

_____

_____

_____

_____

_____

_____

_____

_____

_____

_____

_____

_____

_____

_____

_____

_____

Workbook: The Rebirth and Revival of a Rebel

_____

_____

_____

_____

_____

_____

_____

_____

_____

_____

_____

_____

_____

_____

_____

_____

_____

_____

_____

_____

_____

_____

_____

_____

_____

_____

_____

_____

STEP ONE: The Power Of Confirming

- Confirming is a powerful psychological tool created by educator and spiritual teacher Alain Yaovi M Dagba that is used with a neutral person to play the role of the person who has hurt you in the past to confirm your power and ability to create the better future you have imagined for yourself and written down. This technique will further the redesigning of the new neuropathways inside the brain using new positive data.

Facilitator: Jean Belizaire

Description:

Once the participants realize that the past exists only inside their brain, and that they have the power to reverse it, a neutral person will be chosen to play the role of their father, or mother, or any of the subjects that has hurt them to confirm the new lifestyle they want to live. Since the brain works by association and cannot tell the difference between what is imagined and what is happening in real time, it will replace the created through roleplaying and confirming. This is the real path to forgiveness.

Workshop Setting:

Through a strategic art of group participation and storytelling Pastor Jean Belizaire will be helping the audience or participants go through the power of revers psychology that brings a mental liberation and an emotional freedom.

Workshop Tools:

- Active Creating
- Body relaxation
- Reading the best version of the future
- Roleplaying

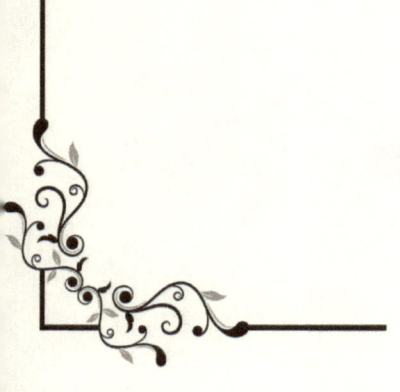

Jean Belizaire

ACTIVE CREATING

What type of lifestyle would you create for
yourself now that you know you deserve to live
and give yourself the best thing in life?

What do you see yourself owning?
What type of family do you see yourself having?
How much money do you see yourself earning?
What are some of the humanitarian
assistances you can give others?
What type of house are you living in?
What type of car are you driving?
What are some of the places you are visiting
all around the world?
How can you pay this experience of positive
transformation forward to others?

Confirming

Recall the image of your father and mother
and assume they are the ones standing in front
of you telling you how possible it is for you to
achieve the lifestyle you have written down as
the best version of the future you desire to have.

A Neutral Person Will Roleplay

Workbook: The Rebirth and Revival of a Rebel

PS: it's important that the confirming portion is done with the participation of the crowd following instructions given by the workshop leader: Jean Belizaire

_____
_____
_____
_____
_____
_____
_____
_____
_____
_____
_____
_____
_____
_____
_____
_____
_____
_____
_____
_____
_____
_____
_____

Jean Belizaire

Workbook: The Rebirth and Revival of a Rebel

Jean Belizaire

Workbook: The Rebirth and Revival of a Rebel

_____

_____

_____

_____

_____

_____

_____

_____

_____

_____

_____

_____

_____

_____

_____

_____

_____

_____

_____

_____

_____

_____

_____

_____

_____

_____

_____

_____

_____

Jean Belizaire

Workbook: The Rebirth and Revival of a Rebel